D0182520

Witness to History

The D-Day Landings

Sean Connolly

Heinemann
LIBRARY

www.heinemann.co.uk/library

Visit our website to find out more information about **Heinemann Library** books.

To order:

 Phone 44 (0) 1865 888066

 Send a fax to 44 (0) 1865 314091

🖥 Visit the Heinemann Bookshop at www.heinemann.co.uk/library to browse our catalogue and order online.

First published in Great Britain by Heinemann Library,
Halley Court, Jordan Hill, Oxford
OX2 8EJ, part of Harcourt Education.

Heinemann is a registered trademark of
Harcourt Education Ltd.

Produced for Heinemann by Discovery Books Ltd
Editorial: Sarah Eason and Gill Humphrey
Design: Ian Winton
Picture Research: Gill Humphrey and Rachel Tisdale
Production: Edward Moore

Originated by Ambassador Litho Ltd
Printed and bound in Hong Kong, China
by South China Printing

ISBN 0 431 17043 6
07 06 05 04 03
10 9 8 7 6 5 4 3 2 1

British Library Cataloguing in Publication Data
Connolly, Sean
  The D-Day Landings. – (Witness to History)
  940.5'421421

A full catalogue record for this book is available from the
British Library.

Acknowledgements
The publishers would like to thank the following for
permission to reproduce photographs:
Associated Press; p.**32**; Bettmann/Corbis p.**40**; Corbis pp.**4**,
7, **8**, **17**, **23**, **38**, **43**, **50**; Hulton-Deutsch Collection/Corbis
pp.**9**, **44**, **46**; Imperial War Musuem p.**36**; Peter Newark's
Military Pictures p.**45**; Popperfoto pp.**6**, **22**, **26**;
Topham/Associated Press pp.**10**, **14**, **28**, **34**, **42**;
Topham/Photonews p.**19**; Topham Picturepoint pp.**12**, **15**,
16, **24**, **25**, **37**; Topham/PA p.**18**, **20**.

Cover photograph shows US soldiers wading ashore during
the D-Day invasion of Normandy, France, reproduced with
permission of Corbis.

The publishers would like to thank Bob Rees, historian and
assistant head teacher, for his assistance in the preparation
of this book.

Disclaimer
All Internet addresses (URLs) given in this book were
valid at the time of going to press. However, due to the
dynamic nature of the Internet, some addresses may have
changed, or sites may have changed or ceased to exist
since publication. While the author and publisher regret
any inconvenience this may cause readers, no
responsibility for any such changes can be accepted by
either the author or the publisher.

Every effort has been made to contact copyright holders of
any material reproduced in this book. Any omissions will
be rectified in subsequent printings if notice is given to the
publishers.

Words appearing in bold, **like this,** are explained in the Glossary.

Contents

Introduction

World War II was the deadliest conflict in history. It cost millions of lives, made millions more homeless and left many countries crushed by its economic cost. For the countries that fought in it, far more was at stake than simply gaining or losing land. The war decided how people would live in the future, either free to choose their own way of life or forced to live under systems of government that disregarded many basic freedoms.

Military dictatorships

Although World War II was a global conflict, most of the fighting on land took place in Europe, North Africa and the Asian countries bordering the Pacific Ocean. By the beginning of the 1930s **military dictatorships** had gained power in Germany, Japan and Italy. The leaders of these countries wanted to extend their power by invading neighbouring territories. They formed an **alliance** and became known as the **Axis** powers. Germany's ruling **Nazi** Party, led by Adolf Hitler, believed that Germans were superior to other nationalities and therefore had the right to invade and occupy other countries.

Ranged against the Axis powers were the **Allies**, led by Great Britain, the **Soviet Union**, China and, from 1941, the USA. These countries pledged to stop and reverse the advance of the Axis war machines.

German troops march through the Arc de Triomphe into the heart of Paris, the capital city, after France surrendered on 25 June 1940.

The Axis countries made many advances in the first years of the war. Japan swept through much of south and south-east Asia threatening India to the west and Australia to the south. By the time the USA joined the war in 1941, much of mainland Europe was under German control and 3 million German

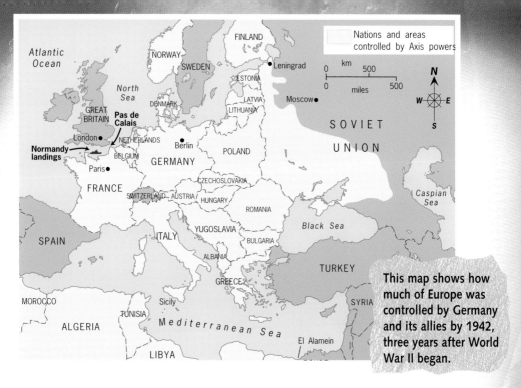

This map shows how much of Europe was controlled by Germany and its allies by 1942, three years after World War II began.

soldiers were pouring into the Soviet Union. The Soviet leader, Josef Stalin, insisted that Great Britain and the USA plan an attack against German-held France. This 'second **front**', he argued, would lessen the pressure on his own country. At the Teheran meeting, in December 1943, the three major Allied leaders, Stalin, British prime minister Winston Churchill and US president Franklin Roosevelt agreed that such an invasion should take place. However, a massive invasion force would be needed if the attack was to be successful.

D-Day and beyond

Early on 6 June 1944, a date since remembered as 'D-Day' (the military code for the 'day' of the invasion) Allied planes began bombing the German coastal defences. **Paratroopers** were dropped inland to cut off German supply routes. Soon after daybreak troops began landing on five French beaches on the Normandy coastline. The fighting was fierce, but by the end of the day each one of the beaches was captured. The Allies were then able to send more troops and equipment to France, using the captured beaches as ports. Over the next few weeks the Germans were driven back from Normandy although the fighting remained bitter. Nearly another year of war lay ahead, but now Germany was on the defensive and it was only a matter of time before the Allies triumphed.

How do we know?

By studying history, we can learn about the events of the past. If we need to find out about, for example, the fall of the Roman Empire or the American Civil War, we can find many books and articles about these subjects. They can tell us when and how these events took place, as well as who were the leading characters. They often go on to explain not only why things have happened, by giving the background to the events, but also how the events themselves changed the course of history. Although these works are helpful and informative, they are often based on **secondary sources**, which are accounts written down some time after the event and by people who were probably not personally involved.

Getting to the source

This book aims to use **primary sources** to tell the story of D-Day. These are the 'first-hand' accounts written down at the time by people who were involved in the events taking place. Historians dealing with events of long ago must rely on written primary sources such as codes of law, parish registers, letters and sometimes journals or diaries. As D-Day is a more recent event there are many people still alive who lived through this period and so historians can use a much

Excited Londoners read the first reports of the D-Day invasion in the newspapers of 6 June 1944.

wider range of primary sources to get at the truth of this story. Tape recordings, online interviews, newspaper reports and film footage of events add personal touches to the wealth of written material we have about this dramatic military victory. While looking at primary sources of this wartime era historians have to remember that **censorship** was imposed on reporting media such as newspapers and the wireless (radio). Even soldiers' letters sent home to their families were opened and any 'sensitive' information was blacked out.

Putting it all together

Not every primary source is objective and that is true of some of the sources you will find in this book. When they are studying sources historians have to be aware of the possible **bias** of the previous writers, which can make some historical accounts unreliable. They have to compare accounts written by different

War reporters, such as America's Ernie Pyle, gave readers a first-hand account of the fighting in their reports sent home from the battlefield.

people and consider the possible **prejudices** the writers might have. For example, if the writer did not like Germans he or she is less likely to give a completely truthful account of them. Furthermore, personal diaries and accounts tell the truth, but only so far as the writer can know it. People in the thick of a battle can only observe what is happening around them, and they sometimes have no clear idea of which side is winning overall. On the other hand, we often know the outcome of a historical event, such as the D-Day invasion, but have little idea of what it was really like to live through it. The primary sources in this book provide a very personal and dramatic picture of one of the most important battles in history.

Early planning

World War II began at different times for different people. In China war came in 1937 when the country was invaded by Japan. For the USA the war did not start until 1941. However, many people think of the war as beginning in 1939 when **Nazi** Germany invaded and occupied Poland. By 1940 many countries, notably France, Belgium, Luxembourg, the Netherlands, Norway and Denmark had been defeated by, or had surrendered to, the Germans. Great Britain repelled the German advance during the Battle of Britain. This took place in 1940 when the British Royal Air Force narrowly defeated the German airforce in the skies over south-east Britain. But the German army remained in control of much of continental Europe, with troops and heavy **artillery** positioned along the north coast of France within just a few miles of Britain. Then, in 1941, the Germans turned to the east, sweeping into the **Soviet Union** with tanks, planes and more than 3 million soldiers. They raced to within 30 kilometres (19 miles) of the capital city, Moscow and surrounded Russia's second most important city, Leningrad.

Great Britain, Germany's only remaining enemy in Western Europe, desperately needed a **strategy** to reverse this string of Nazi triumphs. The USA was not yet in the war. National pride, **morale** and military sense demanded something big. In late 1941 the British Chiefs of Staff ordered Admiral Lord Louis Mountbatten to consider **amphibious** operations in German-controlled Europe.

An aircraft spotter scans the skies over London during the Battle of Britain in 1940. The Germans were trying to gain control of British air space before launching an invasion of Britain.

In October 1941, Prime Minister Winston Churchill summoned Lord Mountbatten back to London to take on a new position. Mountbatten, who had been waiting to take command of the aircraft carrier HMS *Illustrious* in the Pacific Ocean, was worried that he would be offered a boring 'desk job'. Instead, Churchill had something far more dramatic in mind. Mountbatten recorded Churchill's words on 22 October 1941.

You will carry on with the **commando** raids on the occupied coasts of Europe, not only to keep up our morale and to worry the Germans but because I want you to learn the technique of **opposed landings**, for you are to prepare for the invasion of Europe. We cannot win this war unless we land an army in France and defeat Hitler on land. You must arrange to collect soldiers, sailors and airmen, put them in training-bases, teach them to operate as one force. You must devise the new techniques, you must design new landing-craft, new landing-ships, the equipment and the appliances necessary for invasion. The whole of the South of England is a **bastion** of defence against Hitler's invasion. You must turn that into a springboard for our own attack. Every other headquarters in England is thinking defensively, yours is to think only offensively.

Admiral Lord Louis Mountbatten shortly after being appointed as Britain's Chief of Combined Forces in 1941.

The USA enters the war

On 7 December 1941, the Japanese bombed the US Pacific fleet moored at Pearl Harbor on the island of Hawaii, so bringing the USA into the war on the side of the **Allies**. The Pacific region immediately became an important area of fighting, but US forces also became involved in fighting the **Axis** powers in Europe and North Africa. US Major-General Dwight Eisenhower was chosen as Supreme Allied Commander in 1942, but soon found that the Americans and British disagreed about when and where to fight the Germans. Eisenhower and other senior Americans wanted to wait until 1943 and then attack German-controlled Europe directly. Senior British officials, believing that US forces lacked combat experience, wanted to attack a '**flank**' earlier, in 1942. The British already had some combat experience under the command of General Bernard Law Montgomery who had won a stirring victory against the Germans at El Alamein, in Egypt, in October 1942.

In late 1942, Eisenhower led the Allies in Operation Torch in North Africa, which was the USA's first real land warfare experience against the Germans. After a series of setbacks against the brilliant German general, Erwin Rommel, the Allies drove the Germans from North Africa in May 1943. Eisenhower was promoted to the rank of full general. Two months later the Allies landed in Sicily and began a long and difficult campaign northwards through Italy.

Cheering crowds welcomed US troops after Allied forces had captured Palermo, Sicily's largest city, on 18 October 1943.

Dean McCandless remembers his first days in occupied Sicily

Dean McCandless, a US **paratrooper**, was among the first Allied soldiers to set foot in Sicily. German forces were all around, but he managed to link up with other US soldiers. Many months of tough fighting would lie ahead, but the experience would help Allied commanders plan the D-Day invasion less than a year later.

On the night of July 9, 1943 we jumped into Sicily. I landed near our intended drop zone, though we didn't know it at the time. Once out of my parachute, I soon located one of my men, Ott Carpenter, and we were joined by another half dozen troopers.

We went up the road until we ran into a machine-gun nest and scattered. Where everyone went, I'll never know but Ott and I remained together. Not knowing where we were, we decided to do what we had been instructed to do in that situation – head for the highest ground we could see. We ... got to the top of a small mountain by dawn...

When evening shadows began appearing, we began to work our way toward our own lines. It was near day break when I tripped over a gun muzzle extending out from some shrubs ... I jumped past it and shoved the muzzle of my rifle into the chest of a drowsy outpost soldier who shouted 'God almighty don't shoot!' His southern drawl was music to our ears and the stress and tension of two nights and a day vanished.

Building up a force

With Americans fighting alongside the **Allies**, the war had entered a new phase and **morale** rose considerably. The USA had enormous industrial power, capable of producing large quantities of ships, weapons and fuel. Its population of more than 130 million – almost three times that of Great Britain – would provide many soldiers.

Throughout 1942, 1943 and 1944, **convoys** of US ships were sent to aid the Allied cause in Europe. The destination for the US troops and equipment was Great Britain. Some were sent on to North Africa and later Italy as part of Operation Husky, but many more remained in Great Britain. The British public largely welcomed the **GIs**, although some British men envied the Americans' better pay and equipment – and their popularity with British women! With all these soldiers about it was becoming obvious that the Americans and British, along with troops from other Allied countries, were preparing for a major operation. There was a sense of anticipation in the air, but the public had no idea of where or when such an operation would take place.

Private Gordon Carson recalls his excitement at being in wartime London
Private Gordon Carson was one of the thousands of US soldiers who had arrived in Great Britain in the months leading up to the Normandy invasion. Like other Allied soldiers, he felt that he was part of an historic episode in world history. Here he describes the sense of excitement and anticipation that filled the British capital city during the long build-up to the great invasion.

London to me was a magic carpet. Walk down any of its streets and every uniform of the Free World was to be seen. Their youth and vigour vibrated in every park and pub. To Piccadilly, Hyde Park, Leicester Square, Trafalgar Square, Victoria they came. The uniform of the Canadians, South Africans, Australians, New Zealanders, the Free French, Polish, Belgians, Dutch and of course the English and Americans were everywhere. Those days were not lost on me because even at twenty years of age, I knew I was seeing and being a part of something that was never to be again. Wartime London was its own world.

Huge arrays of field guns and other military equipment were stored at secret locations across the British countryside during the build-up to the D-Day invasion.

A solemn promise

The leaders of the three major **Allied** powers, Franklin Roosevelt, Winston Churchill and Josef Stalin, met for four days at the end of 1943 in Teheran, the capital of Iran. They wanted to decide on a **strategy** for fighting the **Axis** powers in Europe. Everyone agreed that they needed to attack, but the question was where and when? Stalin believed that his country, the **Soviet Union**, had been bearing an overwhelming share of the Allied defence against Hitler. The average number of Soviet soldiers and citizens dying every day trying to defeat the Germans was around 19,000 (20 million Soviet citizens and soldiers would have perished by the end of the conflict). He therefore insisted on a 'second **front**' – a full-scale Allied assault on Western Europe.

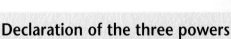

German troops had captured large parts of the western Soviet Union by late 1943, when the three main Allied leaders met in Teheran.

The result of the conference was a spirited statement of the determination and unity of the Allies. It was agreed that the invasion of Europe should take place during May 1944 and that the Soviets would launch an attack at the same time to prevent the Germans from moving their forces away from the **Eastern Front**. Behind the scenes though, Roosevelt and Churchill knew that they had to come up with an invasion plan. Within days US General, Dwight Eisenhower was made Supreme Commander of the Allied Expeditionary Force in Europe. He would be responsible for uniting the commanders of several nationalities and mounting a full-scale invasion of Western Europe. The invasion was given the code name Operation Overlord.

Declaration of the three powers
The official statement at the end of the four-day conference in Teheran masked most of the disagreements and tension of the meeting. The three leaders knew the importance of building **morale** among Allied troops. The rousing words of 1 December 1943 were intended to raise their confidence and to send a clear signal to Germany that the Allies were united.

We the President of the United States, the Prime Minister of Great Britain, and the Premier of the Soviet Union, have met these four days past, in this, the Capital of our Ally, Iran, and have shaped and confirmed our common policy.

We express our determination that our nations shall work together in war and in the peace that will follow.

As to war - our military staffs have joined in our round table discussions, and we have concerted our plans for the destruction of the German forces. We have reached complete agreement as to the scope and timing of the operations to be undertaken from the east, west and south.

The common understanding which we have here reached guarantees that victory will be ours ... No power on earth can prevent our destroying the German armies by land, their U Boats [submarines] by sea, and their war planes from the air ... Our attack will be relentless and increasing...

We came here with hope and determination. We leave here, friends in fact, in spirit and in purpose.

ROOSEVELT, CHURCHILL and STALIN

Signed at Teheran, 1 December 1943

Hitler's role

Germany's military leaders knew that it was only a matter of time before the **Allies** launched some sort of major attack from Britain, aimed at coastal France. But the questions remained: where in France would it be, and how should Germany prepare for it? The German leaders believed that the attack would come from across the Pas de Calais (see map page 5) because here the Channel was narrowest. Naturally the Germans had this area heavily defended. The alternative invasion site was Normandy, which was less well defended. From the Allied viewpoint Normandy, with its broad sandy beaches, was ideal for landing a large invasion force, and the port of Cherbourg could be used to bring in supplies (see map page 30).

Erwin Rommel (left) and Gerd von Rundstedt were in charge of German military preparations for the expected Allied attack on German-held France in 1944.

Gerd von Rundstedt, overall commander of Germany's forces on the **Western Front**, believed that it would be impossible to range powerful forces along all of the 4000-kilometre (2500-mile) French coastline. He preferred to keep most of Germany's forces inland, near Paris, ready to move quickly to whichever spot the Allies chose to invade. Erwin Rommel, who commanded Germany's forces in northern France and Belgium, disagreed. He believed that most of Germany's troops and equipment should be lined along the coast, behind an 'Atlantic Wall' of **artillery** posts, machine-gun nests and other defensive structures.

Both leaders knew that Germany could choose only one of these approaches, because so many German soldiers were already fighting against **Soviet** troops on the **Eastern Front**. But the ultimate choice belonged to the German leader Adolf Hitler, who often issued orders that showed he had no real understanding of the problems involved.

Guenther Blumentritt's memoirs

Guenther Blumentritt, von Rundstedt's chief of staff, was aware of the disagreement between his own superior and Rommel over how to prepare for an Allied attack. His **memoirs** describe their differing approaches and the role played by Adolf Hitler himself in the planning.

Hitler agreed in general with both these reports ... To be sure, he held fast to the immediate defence of the coast in the Rommel sense, but agreed to the formation of Western Command reserves around Paris. But these – since fresh divisions were no longer available – were to consist of **panzer** divisions from the east in need of overhaul ... Hitler's tendency to overrate the value of the defence systems and fortifications ... was generally known. He believed, or imagined, that a blue line along the coast with lots of fortifications ... would completely seal off any attacker. **Illusory** planning maps, were contemplated on the map table! They have a calming effect on those with a flair for fantasy. But such people would have been unpleasantly surprised could they have seen on the spot how poor and thin this 'garrison' really was. Hitler's preference for steel, concrete and iron, and the growing anxiety over the offensive that was being prepared by the Allies ... led him to dream of banishing misfortune by pure defence.

Adolf Hitler, known as 'der Führer' (the Leader), commanded complete obedience from the German people, including Germany's military leaders.

A phantom army

One of the most important **Allied** weapons in the build-up to D-Day was **intelligence**. Members of the French **Resistance** risked their lives to send information about German military preparations to Allied headquarters. They also destroyed bridges and railway lines that the Germans needed to send supplies of ammunition to the coast. A crucial breakthrough came when the British cracked the secret code that the Germans themselves used for all their messages. The British code-breaking operation, known as Ultra, provided the Allies with the latest information about where and when the Germans would move troops and equipment.

The next step was to trick the Germans about the nature of the invasion itself. The Allies knew

Brenda Webb describes how codes were cracked at Bletchley Park

The British Navy captured a German Enigma code-making machine in 1941. The codes were supposedly unbreakable, but top mathematicians working at Bletchley Park, north of London, eventually cracked the codes. Eighteen-year-old Brenda Webb was part of the top-secret British intelligence that helped 'decode' many German messages.

that the Germans expected the attack to come across the Pas de Calais. They decided to play on this mistaken belief by setting up a non-existent 'army' in south-east England in early 1944. George Patton, one of the most famous US generals, was given command of this 'phantom army'. Fake army camps, built from canvas and plywood, sprang up in this area, along with inflatable tanks and mock ships. Deliberately false radio messages, which the Allies knew the Germans would overhear, added to the deception. And thanks to the Ultra system, the Allies knew that their trick was working.

Germany's Enigma code-making machine looked like a typewriter, but messages typed into it could be jumbled up to make it difficult for the Allies to understand.

We were told never ever to tell anyone about it, not your boyfriend, parents, anyone ... With Enigma, any message could be easily translated into groups of five letters, transmitted in **Morse code** and then decoded by the machine using the same settings. The difficulty of the task facing us can be gauged from the number of settings for an Enigma machine – 150 million million million.

Good intelligence work, educated guesses and mind-numbing thoroughness, combined with sloppy German operators, meant signals could be decoded in days or hours.

Much of it depended on the mathematical probability of a particular letter occurring, so machines were built enabling **decryption** that took days manually to be done in half an hour. In fact they developed the world's first programmable computer, but like everything at Bletchley, it remained a secret and its designers, notably mathematician Alan Turing, never received credit for their work.

The peace and quiet of Bletchley Park, a country house north of London, provided an ideal setting for British experts trying to discover the secrets of Germany's Enigma code-making system.

The pressure builds

The build-up to D-Day was incredibly complicated, involving hundreds of aircraft, some 5000 ships and more than 170,000 soldiers. It all had to go like clockwork with the invasion forces sweeping across the Channel from southern England and overwhelming German positions in coastal France. By the spring of 1944 **Allied commandos** had made many secret missions to Normandy to inspect the invasion beaches and to check on German defences.

Meanwhile troops stationed in England began to rehearse their roles in a series of drills and 'dry runs'. Secrecy was to be maintained at all times and **civilians** living in the southern counties often came across notices outside troop camps which read 'DO NOT TALK TO THE TROOPS'. In April 1944 one of these rehearsals ended tragically when some landing-ships ran into German E-Boats (small, fast torpedo boats) and two vessels were sunk, killing 639 US soldiers. Exercise Eagle, the US 101st Airborne Division's rehearsal for the whole operation, took place on 9–12 May 1944, less than a month before the scheduled attack. It involved rehearsals of **paratroop** drops – one of the key elements of the planned invasion. Some parts of this rehearsal failed miserably, with troops separated from each other and nowhere near their planned meeting points. Although most of this and other Allied exercises did go according to plan, the soldiers began to realize that there would be no room for error when the real invasion took place.

The Slapton Sands (Devon) 'dry run' for the Normandy invasion turned into a disaster. Due to a series of mistakes more than 700 died in several incidents that saw soldiers being drowned, accidentally shot or hit by rocket fire.

Alan Moorehead writes

Alan Moorehead, an Australian living in Britain, became a war correspondent for the *Daily Express* newspaper. Unlike the soldiers he followed across the channel on D-Day, he was able to go where he chose, gathering information to send back to Great Britain. Directly after the war he wrote a book about his experiences. This excerpt shows the mood of the country shortly before the landings took place.

The waiting in Britain had gone on so long. The mystery and secrecy of the operation made it more difficult. Although there was a general certainty that the landing would occur, people were without the technical knowledge of how it would be done … All that one could see ahead was a deliberately planned massacre. It would have been much easier if they could have watched the preparations; the submarines stealing in to chart the coast and the seabed; the commandos landing on the beaches to gather information; the hundreds of boats collecting in the ports; the five thousand aircraft preparing for the day …

A dead, heavy mood settled over the country, and this was communicated to the army. Having prepared so long, so thoroughly … it seemed on some black days that one thing would be lacking - the spirit to put the plan into operation … May turned into June. Surely it could not be much longer now. Standing on the South Downs one could see the English Channel, bright and clear and calm. It was hot … the country never looked more calm and beautiful.

The strain of command

The tensions and concerns in the lead-up to D-Day affected everyone involved with the huge operation. The man in charge of the entire operation, US General Dwight D. Eisenhower, known by his nickname 'Ike', was a popular leader with his soldiers and impressed the British with his combination of friendly charm and decisiveness. With his quick smile and easy-going manner, he seemed to typify the values that the **Allies** were fighting to preserve: friendship, compassion and loyalty.

Behind the scenes, though, Eisenhower was feeling the strain. He smoked heavily and found it hard to sleep. The news about the German defences along the French coast made planning complicated. The Germans had laid metal stakes and other obstacles to block the landing of boats and equipment. They were just under water and impossible to see at high tide. If the attack came at low tide, then thousands of Allied soldiers would be sitting targets for German machine guns. Eisenhower knew that the invasion force would need to land at **half tide**. The timing of the invasion had become even more critical.

Eisenhower found he sometimes had to **reprimand** his own generals. General George Patton, who had proved himself a successful and popular leader, already had an unfriendly relationship with General Montgomery. The success of the invasion depended on good relations between Great Britain and the USA, especially at the highest level. Eisenhower could not risk endangering this precious relationship.

General Montgomery (in front), commander of Britain's forces in Western Europe, and (to Montgomery's right) US General Dwight Eisenhower, Supreme Allied Commander, oversee British-American preparations in early 1944.

General Eisenhower's letter to General George Patton

In April 1944, General Patton offended the British with some ill-chosen remarks made near his base in Cheshire, England. Here is an extract from the letter Eisenhower sent to him on 29 April 1944.

*I have warned you time and again against your **impulsiveness** and have flatly instructed you to say nothing that could possibly be misinterpreted. You first came into my command at my own insistence because I believed in your fighting qualities and your ability to lead troops in battle. At the same time I have always been fully aware of your habit of dramatizing yourself and of committing **indiscretions** for no other apparent purpose than of calling attention to yourself. I am thoroughly weary of your failure to control your tongue and have begun to doubt your all-around judgment, so essential in high military position. My decision in the present case will not become final until I have heard from the **War Department**. I want to tell you officially and definitely that if you are again guilty of any indiscretion in speech or action. I will relieve you instantly from command.*

General Patton was a clever, but hot-headed soldier whose tactless remarks offended the British. Nevertheless he played an important role in directing US troops in Normandy in 1944.

German preparations

Although the **Allies** had superior air power and an element of surprise in choosing exactly where the attack would take place, the Germans had other advantages. Even in 1944 the German war machine was very strong, with weapons that were as good as, if not better than, those of the Allies. No one could question the fact that Germany had successful and experienced soldiers. Another advantage was their control of land communications – trains and trucks (though they still also relied on horses). These could carry troops and equipment far more easily than ships. Despite some disagreements about how best to defend against the Allied attack the Germans had a large labour force to carry out their plans.

Begun in 1942, prisoners from Germany's European victories were put to work building a line, about 3800 kilometres (2400 miles) long, of forts and gun emplacements along the west coast of France. The Germans called this line of defence the 'Atlantic Wall'. Its job was to drive back Allied invaders on the beaches themselves, making it impossible to gain a foothold on the continent. Armoured units, using Germany's feared Panther and Tiger **panzers**, could rush to back up any part of the Wall that faced Allied attack. Hitler had once boasted that this defence line was '**impregnable** against every enemy'. Though, as the success of the landings was to show, his confidence in the Wall defences was misplaced.

The Germans placed metal spikes, most of them under water at high tide, along many French beaches to prevent Allied landing craft from reaching the shore.

Major Hans von Luck's memoirs

In May 1944 Major Hans von Luck was given command of a panzer regiment based near the city of Caen, Normandy. In this extract from his **memoirs**, Luck reports the welcome he received from General Edgar Feuchtinger, his superior officer in the region.

Our division is the only one near the coast behind the Atlantic Wall, which, here in Normandy, is not yet fully developed and manned by an inexperienced **infantry** division. The anticipated Allied landing is not expected in Normandy, but rather in the Pas de Calais, the shortest distance between England and the Continent. But Caen, as an important industrial city, is also a key point. That is why it was decided to move a panzer division here by the Atlantic Wall. All the same, we have to reckon on airborne landings or large-scale **commando** operations, which would serve as a diversion from the actual landing. For that reason, Rommel considers it very important that the division should take up combat positions even in the hinterland [land lying behind a coastal region].

Our division has strict orders not to intervene in the event of enemy landings until cleared by Army Group B. Rommel wants all units to make themselves familiar with the terrain – also by night – and regular combat exercises to be carried out. I hope, my dear Luck, that you will be happy with us and I wish you lots of luck.

Huge guns, protected in concrete **bunkers**, formed the backbone of Germany's 'Atlantic Wall' defence against an expected Allied invasion.

'OK, let's go'

Tides and ocean currents played a huge part in the scheduling of the D-Day attack. The biggest concern was the weather. The target date was 5 June, but the weather deteriorated as the day approached. Would the planes be able to fly? Would all the soldiers become seasick before even landing? Would gales blow landing craft back out to sea or even sink them? These were some of the risks if the weather did not improve. However, there would be an almost unbearable two-week wait if the attack was delayed by more than a day.

Senior **Allied** generals and admirals decided to wait an extra day and then to discuss whether to go ahead with the invasion. In the early hours of 5 June 1944 they met again. The wind blew sheets of rain against the windows while **meteorologist** J.M. Stagg announced that the weather would improve briefly on 6 June. Eisenhower then took a poll among those present. Opinion was divided, so the decision rested on Eisenhower's shoulders. He decided that the landings would go ahead, on the morning of 6 June 1944. 'OK, let's go', Ike's words at 4 a.m. on 5 June 1944, set in motion the greatest military attack in history. There would be no turning back.

Long lines of US tanks stop on their way to board invasion ships in southern England in early June 1944.

Eisenhower's orders to the soldiers

General Eisenhower composed a stirring 'Order of the Day', which each soldier taking part in Operation Overlord received on 5 June 1944. In it he summed up the hopes of everyone who prayed for the defeat of Hitler's **Nazi** government.

Soldiers, Sailors and Airmen of the Allied Expeditionary Forces: You are about to embark upon the Great Crusade, toward which we have striven these many months. The eyes of the world are upon you. The hopes and prayers of liberty-loving people everywhere march with you. In company with our brave Allies and brothers-in-arms on other **Fronts** you will bring about the destruction of the German war machine, the elimination of Nazi **tyranny** over **oppressed** peoples of Europe, and security for ourselves in a free world.

Your task will not be an easy one. Your enemy is well trained, well equipped and battle-hardened. He will fight savagely.

But this is the year 1944! Much has happened since the Nazi triumphs of 1940-41. The United Nations have inflicted upon the Germans great defeats, in open battle, man-to-man. Our air offensive has seriously reduced their strength in the air and their capacity to wage war on the ground. Our Home Fronts have given us an overwhelming superiority in weapons and **munitions** of war, and placed at our disposal great reserves of trained fighting men. The tide has turned! The free men of the world are marching together to Victory!

I have full confidence in your courage, devotion to duty and skill in battle. We will accept nothing less than full victory!

Good Luck! And let us all beseech the blessing of Almighty God upon this great and noble undertaking.

Seeing them off

The departure of the D-Day invasion force was dramatic. On 5 June thousands of **Allied** ships of all kinds, including battleships, cruisers, **mine-sweepers**, landing craft, hospital ships and ammunition ships, gathered in the blustery waters of the English Channel. That night hundreds of planes, carrying over twenty thousand **paratroopers**, thundered overhead, all heading in the same direction – south. The months of planning, all the drills and exercises, were over. In order to reach the French coast by the early morning **half tide** all the troop ships had to leave English ports under cover of darkness. The largest invasion in history had begun.

The British public, especially those living in southern England where most of the troops had been stationed, knew that an historic moment had arrived. Even the foreign troops who had been training in England – the Americans, Canadians and South Africans and other Allies – had become part of the English social scene. The number of US fighting men based in Great Britain had doubled in the first six months of 1944, rising from 774,000 at the beginning of the year to 1,537,000 in the week preceding the final assault. Now many of them had gone, and some people wondered when, or if, they would ever see them again.

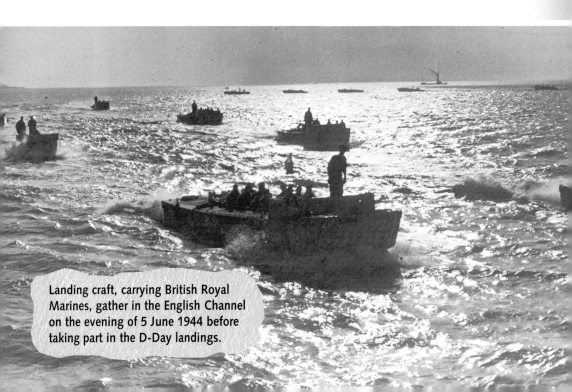

Landing craft, carrying British Royal Marines, gather in the English Channel on the evening of 5 June 1944 before taking part in the D-Day landings.

An English housewife remembers

Weymouth was one of the southern English ports that acted as a 'launch pad' for the Allied invasion. In this extract, a Weymouth housewife describes her sudden sense of loss when she noticed the empty harbour on the morning of 6 June 1944. The invasion force had left in the night.

That Tuesday morning – the 6th – I remember looking out to sea to the spot that the Yanks called 'Piccadilly Corner' because it was there that the landing craft always congregated on the training exercises. And it was empty. For the first time in six months I couldn't see a ship, where there had always been scores of them. They'd gone, the Yanks, and we knew where. I thought of my friend Al who was with the US 1st **Infantry** Division and wondered at that moment where he was now and how he was getting on and whether I'd ever see him again. Then ... I spotted one of those daft little signs that the Yanks chalked up everywhere that year ... It was a drawing of a fat-nosed, stupid-looking chap peering over a wall with the words printed below, KILROY WUZ HERE. I don't know what it was supposed to mean and have never found out. But at that moment it got me. I wasn't very flighty or particularly silly in those days, but for me it seemed to say that my Al had come and gone and like the rest of the Yanks, wouldn't come back. *Kilroy wuz here*, I thought, and burst into tears.

In the air

General Eisenhower was sure that superior **Allied** airpower would be decisive in Operation Overlord. This advantage had already helped prepare the way for the invasion. British and US planes had prevented German reconnaissance aircraft (spy planes) from getting a true picture of the preparations in southern England. They had also destroyed many transport lines and fortifications in France before the attack took place. British and American air crews were aided greatly in targeting their attacks by information sent by the French **Resistance**.

Now, with the attack under way, the air crews knew that their job was to help the massive troop and equipment landings at five Normandy beaches, code-named Juno, Gold, Sword, Utah and Omaha. British troops landed at Sword and Gold, Canadian troops landed at Juno; troops from these three beaches were expected to join together soon after the landing. Americans were landing at Utah and Omaha. Some planes dropped thousands of **paratroopers** beyond the German coastal defences Others towed gliders (carrying guns and vehicles) and sent them on their way to the same destination. Still others continued their pre-invasion job of pounding the German **artillery** posts with powerful bombs. On the same night the French Resistance themselves carried out over 1000 **sabotage** attacks against rail-links and other lines of communication.

This map shows part of the northern coastline of France, and the position of the Normandy beaches where the D-Day landings took place.

James Delong remembers his first mission of the D-Day operation

James Delong was a crew member of an American B-26 bomber which attacked German coastal artillery sites in the hours before the D-Day landings. His crew had already flown fifty-five missions over Europe, but the night of 5–6 June 1944 was the first time they would take off in darkness.

On June 6, we woke at 01.30. We knew that this was the day; this was the hour we had been waiting for ... Boy, it's dark and rainy. We're not accustomed to this at all; we've done only daylight missions. Time to fire the engines ... We have a climb pattern, but no time for practice. It's got to be perfect the first time. Throttles wide open, and off we go ... The sky was full of planes, and below, the water was covered with surface vessels. We expected to see German fighters as we neared the coast, but didn't. As we approached the target, the bomb-bay doors opened and 'Bombs away!' There was light **flak** coming up, and the bombardier said we got a good hit. Out over the French countryside, scattered everywhere, were parachutes and pieces of huge crashed gliders. I don't believe I saw an undamaged one. I had this sick feeling that things were not going well.

We made a sweeping turn back to the coast and the formation tightened, and I could see aircraft everywhere approaching the coast. We flew back over the sea full of vessels and made landfall over the white cliffs at Beachy Head [on the Sussex Coast], and then around the London balloons to our base. We made another flight later in the day.

31

The first fighting

Allied aircraft flew over the Normandy coast in the early hours of 6 June 1944. Once past the German coastal defences, they dropped thousands of **paratroopers** who had an important role to play if the invasion was to be a success. These men had to capture bridges, railway lines and roads that the Germans would use for communication and reinforcements once the Allied landing force reached the beaches.

Parachute training was difficult and intense. The men knew that they ran a high risk of being killed or captured once the operation began. Some of the paratroopers were shot while floating down; others got tangled in trees or wires. Still others landed safely, but well away from their intended targets – and from their fellow soldiers. Despite these difficulties, the Allied paratroopers did gain control of many roads and railway lines. The British captured the Merville **Battery**, near the mouth of the River Orne (see map page 30). The US 82nd Division secured an important road junction at Ste Mere Eglise (between Utah and Omaha beaches). These early successes were vital, preventing German tanks positioned at Caen from moving east and crushing the invasion before the troops could get off the beaches. For the first time in four years, Allied soldiers were fighting the Germans on French soil. The battle had begun.

Tension is written on the faces of these US paratroopers as they fly across the English Channel on their way to Normandy on 6 June 1944.

Sergeant Thornton fires an important shot

Sergeant 'Wagger' Thornton was a member of the British 6th Airborne Division, which landed by the River Orne in Normandy on 6 June. They encountered fierce German resistance after they had captured the vital Pegasus Bridge over the river. The PIAT (an anti-tank grenade launcher) shot that he describes here was the most important shot in this particular fight, as it forced German troops to retreat and prevented tanks from stopping the Sword beach landings.

The tanks were making their way down probably to recapture the bridge, and Howard asked Fox if he had a PIAT, and I suddenly found myself entrusted with the PIAT. I took a chap with me, to be a number 2, and off we went.

Now a PIAT is a load of rubbish really. First, you're a dead loss if you have to go even 50 yards, and second, you must never, never miss. If you do, you've had it, because by the time you reload the thing and cock it, which is a chore on its own, everything is gone. You're **indoctrinated** into your brain that you mustn't miss. So, I lay down with this other guy about 30 yards from the T-junction of the road. I was shaking like a leaf. Sure enough, in about three minutes this tank appears, the old wheels were rattling away, and I could more hear it than see it. I took aim, and although shaking, bang, and off it went. The thing exploded right bang in the middle, and a couple of minutes later, all hell let loose. I was so excited and shaking, and I had to move back a bit. Two or three guys jumped out of the thing, and I said to my number 2 to give them a few bursts from the Sten [machine gun] which he did.

The German response

All through the beginning of 1944, while the **Allied** invasion force had been preparing for the D-Day landings, the German forces ranged along the French coast had been going through their own drills and exercises. Each soldier knew exactly what he needed to do – and where he needed to be – when the invaders arrived.

But as Allied planes began their bombing runs over Normandy before dawn on 6 June 1944, the Germans were shocked. The troops stationed there, like nearly all Germans, had expected that the invasion would take place farther to the north, near Calais. While the bombs rained down on the Normandy stretch of Germany's 'Atlantic Wall', the Germans began getting reports of **paratroopers** landing further inland. The months of preparations would now need to be put into practice, but the massive air attack warned them of the hard fighting that lay ahead.

While some of the troops stationed along the 'Atlantic Wall' were well trained and well equipped, some of the German troops units were poorly equipped and undermanned. As became clear when the Allies began to round up prisoners, many of the German troops were very young – only sixteen or seventeen years old. Some were not even German, but had been **conscripted** into the army from the German-occupied territories in Eastern Europe and the **Soviet Union**.

A German **artillery** soldier, his heavy naval gun half-hidden by trees, waits for the sight of Allied aircraft during the D-Day invasion.

Franz Gockel remembers his feelings of surprise when the Allied bombers appeared

Franz Gockel was a German **infantry** soldier stationed along the coast behind Omaha Beach. Like most other German soldiers along this stretch of French coastline, he had expected the Allied landing for months. But the attack was still a surprise when it took place on 6 June 1944. Gockel soon realized that Allied air power would carry the day.

The alarm call into the **bunker** woke us from a deep sleep ... We had so often been shaken to our feet by this call in the past weeks that we no longer took the alarms seriously, and some of the men rolled over in their bunks and attempted to sleep. An **NCO** brought us to our feet with the words 'Guys, this time it's for real. They're coming!'

We sprang into action ... and ran to our positions. Our coastal section remained quiet – nothing moved. Was it once again a false alarm? The silence weighed heavily upon us and the tension continued to build. Soon the sound of bomber squadrons could be detected in the distance. With the morning dawn came more bombers...

The bombers were suddenly over us and it was too late to spring into the prepared dugout for cover. I dived under the gun as bombs screamed and hissed into the sand and earth. Two heavy bombs fell on our position. Debris and clouds of smoke enveloped us; the earth shook; eyes and nose were filled with dirt, and sand ground between teeth. There was no hope for help. No German aircraft appeared, and this sector had no **anti-aircraft** guns.

Beach combat

The main fighting on D-Day came along the five invasion beaches. Troop ships, along with open-topped, flat-bottomed LCIs (Landing Craft **Infantry**) and LSTs (Landing Ship Tank), carried the soldiers across the Channel. The LCIs, the LSTs and the other smaller landing craft then made the dangerous last leg of the journey into shallower waters close to the beaches, where the soldiers jumped out to wade ashore.

Many British soldiers arrived on the Normandy beaches with bicycles to help them move more quickly once they had got ashore.

Death and destruction seemed to engulf the troops. Their vessels bobbed and swayed in the waves, causing many men to be seasick. Many US troops landing at Utah Beach were slumped down vomiting – or already dead from machine-gun fire – as their landing craft opened their hatches. They were also in the line of German fire – from machine guns and heavier **artillery**. Canadians landing at Juno Beach could see Germans perched in church steeples and other tall buildings, signalling the **Allied** positions to machine gunners on the ground. The British 3rd Division, landing at Sword, found themselves facing the full might of a German tank division. It was up to the Allied soldiers to take cover from this fire wherever they could find it: behind sand dunes, broken equipment or even behind the bodies of fallen soldiers.

Hamilton, a Canadian soldier, remembers

J.H. Hamilton, a Canadian soldier in the Royal Winnipeg Rifles, landed at Juno Beach in the main D-Day invasion. His landing craft lost an engine on the way, leaving the men open to German fire for far longer than they had expected.

There was quite a bit of enemy fire on the coast, and we were being heavily fired upon as we approached ... The lad in front of me was Rifleman Philip Gianelli, and as the ramp went down, he took a burst of machine-gun fire in his stomach, ahead of me, while I wasn't touched by that burst. There was a **tracer** in the burst, and you could see it coming to us, and Gianelli was killed instantly.

I got off the landing craft and crossed the narrow sandy beach to the edge of the beach sand dune. I got some protection, but still, I suffered a piece of **shrapnel** lodged in my right nostril. I was unconscious for some time, and being one of the early waves on the beach, there was no first aid station ... Finally there were five or six walking wounded, and we formed up a section and moved off the beach to follow the route of our company inland, and I went to the village of Sainte-Croix, which our battalion had taken. There were a number of dead Germans lying in the streets.

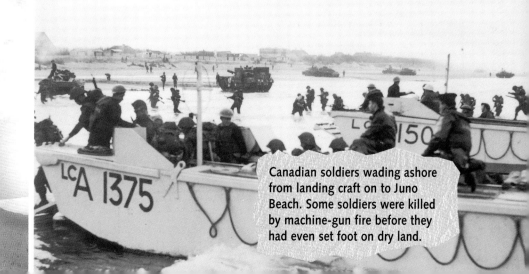

Canadian soldiers wading ashore from landing craft on to Juno Beach. Some soldiers were killed by machine-gun fire before they had even set foot on dry land.

Gaining a foothold

The **Allies** gradually gained control of Juno, Sword, Gold and Utah beaches. The last to be taken was Omaha Beach, one of the two US landing sites. Omaha was always going to be difficult because steep cliffs behind the beach formed a natural wall. Also it was more heavily defended than the Allies had expected. Aerial bombing (taking place from the air) and bombardments from offshore ships had failed to damage the German gun stations looking down on the beach. Worse still, the bad weather turned the waters around Omaha into a heaving mass. US Navy ships launched the landing craft from 19 kilometres (twelve miles) out, rather than the planned 13 kilometres (eight miles). All of these factors combined to make it almost impossible to capture the beach.

The Germans sensed the Americans' dismay and confusion and believed that they could hold on to the beach. German machine guns opened fire on landing craft as soon as they unloaded their troops. The Allies suffered heavily at Omaha with 2500 Americans dead, missing or wounded by nightfall. The beach was only taken because of the planning before the landing itself. The French **Resistance** and Allied bombing had successfully blocked German supply routes. As no extra ammunition could reach the Germans they were forced to withdraw.

Grim clouds form a suitable backdrop for the US troops as they wade ashore at Omaha, the most difficult of the five landing beaches to capture.

William Stanley remembers landing at Omaha beach

Infantryman William J. Stanley was part of the US invasion force that landed on Omaha Beach on the morning of 6 June 1944. His account shows how difficult conditions were at Omaha – even before the men set foot on the beach.

We circled for one and a half hours in the storm, then headed for the beach. One hundred feet [30 metres] from shore, my landing craft hit a sand bar. Thinking we were on the beach, the ramp was dropped, which was a signal to disembark. We ran into twelve feet [3.7 metres] of water. There was widespread panic. The weak and non-swimmers drowned. The war ended for them one hundred feet from the invasion on Omaha Beach. The shock, fear, and reality of what happened is indescribable.

When my feet touched the beach, I made my way to shore, stumbling and pushing bodies of my American comrades aside. There was one way to go – ahead. Gunfire hit the water, and bodies became sandbags and protection. Not one American son could ever be prepared for this. Everything was instinctive and I kept moving ahead.

We huddled behind the sand dunes on the beach while the **artillery** continued firing toward us. The choice was either to huddle there and be killed by gunfire or move forward.

The grim struggle

All through the day of 6 June the fighting continued. Mines and underwater explosives ripped some **Allied** landing craft apart even before they reached the shore. German machine-gun nests picked off soldiers almost at will, often concentrating their fire on officers, whom they could recognize by their uniforms. As a result many groups of soldiers, especially on Omaha beach, found themselves without commanding officers. For them victory seemed like a distant hope. Simply surviving would be the main battle.

Colonel S. A. Marshall, landing with the US forces at Omaha, described what seemed to be a hopeless position as men arrived by landing craft: 'The ramp drops. In that instant, two machine guns concentrate their fire on the opening. Not a man is given time to jump. All aboard are cut down where they stand.'

However, by nightfall on 6 June 1944 it had become clear that the main objective of the D-Day operation – taking the five beaches – had succeeded. But the cost had been great, and it was not yet clear whether the Germans would be pushed back from their stronghold in Normandy.

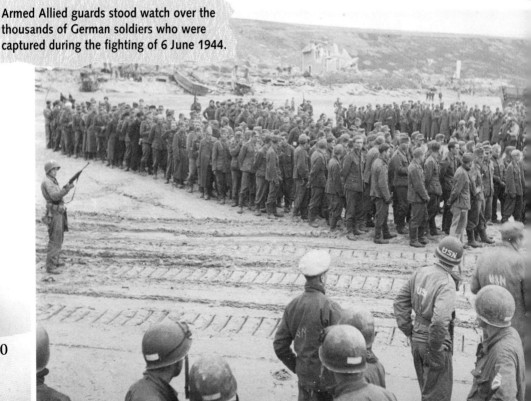

Armed Allied guards stood watch over the thousands of German soldiers who were captured during the fighting of 6 June 1944.

Ernie Pyle was one of the most respected, and best-loved, of America's war reporters. He joined the US forces in Normandy one day after the D-Day landings. His first report paints a vivid picture of a grim and bloody battlefield.

By the time we got here the beaches had been taken and the fighting had moved a couple of miles inland. All that remained on the beach was some sniping and **artillery** fire, and the occasional startling blast of a mine geysering brown sand into the air. That plus a gigantic and pitiful litter of wreckage along miles of shoreline.

Submerged tanks and overturned boats and burned trucks and shell-shattered jeeps and sad little personal belongings were strewn all over these bitter sands. That plus the bodies of soldiers lying in rows covered with blankets, the toes of their shoes sticking up in a line as though on drill. And other bodies, uncollected, still sprawling grotesquely in the sand or half hidden by the high grass beyond the beach.

That, plus an intense, grim determination of work-weary men to get this chaotic beach organized and get all the vital supplies and the reinforcements moving more rapidly over it from the stacked-up ships standing in droves out to sea.

Beyond the call of duty

The fighting on D-Day was a terrible experience for soldiers on both sides. Normal activities, such as eating, sleeping and washing, became almost impossible as troops found themselves in constant danger. Soldiers had to deal with the endless noise of rifle shots, hand grenades and aerial bombing that continued throughout each day and into the night.

But despite these constant dangers, there were many stories of heroism as soldiers risked their own lives to save or protect their fellow troops. Some crawled for many metres across open ground to attack a machine-gun nest that was protected by thick concrete walls. Others dashed along the beach to rescue wounded comrades. Among the most courageous troops were the 'medics', doctors, nurses and assistants who treated the wounded – often in the line of enemy fire.

Military leaders recognized these acts of courage by awarding their most valued medals. Company Sergeant-Major Stanley Hollis of the Green Howards regiment was awarded the Victoria Cross (the highest British military award). Other British and Canadian soldiers were awarded the Distinguished Service Order, while Americans received the Medal of Honor and Silver Star.

Black soldiers from countries such as Tunisia and Guyana (South America) and the USA played an important part in the D-Day landings. Here African American soldiers unload ammunition for the **Allied** soldiers. This was dangerous work often done under German machine-gun fire.

Private Carlton W. Barrett receives the Medal of Honor

This **citation** accompanied the Medal of Honor that was awarded to Private Carlton W. Barrett of the US Army on 2 October 1944, nearly four months after his heroic actions on D-Day. The Medal of Honor is the highest US military award and is reserved for acts of unusual bravery.

Citation:

For gallantry and intrepidity at the risk of his life above and beyond the call of duty on 6 June 1944, in the vicinity of St. Laurent-sur-Mer, France. On the morning of D-Day Pvt. Barrett, landing in the face of extremely heavy enemy fire, was forced to wade ashore through neck-deep water. Disregarding the

Quick thinking and prompt action by 'medics' saved the lives of many soldiers, like this wounded American **infantryman**.

personal danger, he returned to the surf again and again to assist his floundering [struggling] comrades and save them from drowning. Refusing to remain pinned down by the intense **barrage** [constant fire from artillery) of small arms and mortar fire poured at the landing points, Pvt. Barrett, working with fierce determination, saved many lives by carrying casualties to an evacuation boat lying offshore. In addition to his assigned mission as guide, he carried dispatches the length of the fire-swept beach; he assisted the wounded; he calmed the shocked; he arose as a leader in the stress of the occasion. His coolness and his dauntless daring courage while constantly risking his life during a period of many hours had an inestimable effect on his comrades.

French reaction

France had been defeated by Germany in the middle of 1940. The parts of the country that were nearest Great Britain – and therefore the likeliest spots for an **Allied** invasion – were ruled directly by the Germans. Most French people living under this German occupation longed for the day when they would once more be able to govern themselves. Many French people joined the **Resistance**, the movement dedicated to helping to free their country from **Nazi** rule. Their contribution was vital to the success of the D-Day operation. Others, under General Charles de Gaulle, formed the Free French Army, which fought alongside other Allied forces.

On the evening of 5 June, a poem by the French poet Paul Verlaine was broadcast on the BBC's French radio service. This was a signal to the Resistance that the invasion was under way and their planned **sabotage** attacks could begin. Once the invasion force had landed, Resistance members used their knowledge of the local countryside to help ensure **Allied** success.

French resistance fighters, some of them women, planned and implemented many sabotage attacks on German communication lines as the Allied invasion force was approaching the Normandy beaches. Here they are involved in liberating Paris a few months after the D-Day landings.

Many ordinary French people also welcomed the invasion force, providing food and drink to the soldiers who were **liberating** their country. Most knew that the destruction and conflict taking place all around them would lead to German defeat, and they were proud to play their part in the struggle. Others, particularly those who had lost their homes and farms or who saw their home town or city destroyed by the allied bombing, were less overjoyed.

Mademoiselle Genget's diary

Mlle Genget lived in the village of St-Come-de-Fresne, near the D-Day invasion beach named Gold. Her diary entry on 6 June 1944 reflects her joy and excitement as it becomes clear that the long-awaited invasion has taken place on her own doorstep.

What seemed impossible has really happened! The English have landed on the French coast and our little village has become famous in a few hours! Not one **civilian** killed or wounded. How can we express our surprise after such long years of waiting in wonderment and fear?...

What a sight met our eyes [from a nearby cliff]! As far as we could see there were ships of all kinds and sizes and above floated big balloons silvery in the sun. Big bombers were passing and re-passing in the sky. As far as Courseulles [further along the coast] one could see nothing but ships.

Is it all really true? We are at last liberated. The enormous strength that all this war represents is fantastic, and the way it has been handled with such precision is marvellous ... A group of Tommies [nickname for the British soldiers] pass and ask us for water. We fill their bottles, say a few words, and, having given chocolates and sweets to the children, they continue on their way.

An August 1944 poster celebrating the work of the French Resistance. The words announce that members of the Resistance had 'poured out their blood for the people of Paris'.

45

D-Day plus

Each day after the landings was known as 'Day-Day plus 1', 'D-Day plus 2' and so forth. On 11 June, just a few days after the landings, Hitler issued the order that there was to be 'no retreat' and German soldiers were forced to carrying on fighting against this massive **Allied** attack. By 'D-Day plus 23' the Allies had not advanced far into France, although there were 850,000 Allied troops and 150,000 vehicles ashore in Normandy. The German defence still made it hard for the two main groups of Allies – British/Canadian and American – to join forces.

British troops concentrated on the heavily defended city of Caen near Juno, Gold and Sword beaches (see map page 30). At the end of June, in an attack code named 'Operation Epsom', a large-scale Allied **infantry** force attacked west of Caen. It was unsuccessful and resulted in 4000 men being killed or wounded. Then General Montgomery, commander-in-chief of the British forces, began 'Operation Goodwood', designed to take on German forces in a large tank battle to the east of Caen. Despite heavy bombing by Allied planes, Operation Goodwood showed no sign of succeeding even by mid-July. The prolonged British struggle near Caen did, however, begin to have an effect. The Germans were using up precious troops and equipment. With German tanks concentrated around Caen, the American forces found it easier to capture the important port of Cherbourg.

Lieutenant John Brown's experiences

Lieutenant John Brown, from the British infantry, describes an Allied bombing raid on Caen on 7 July 1944, in the middle of Operation Goodwood. The attack, however, did little to dislodge the Germans from their strongholds in and around the city.

As we lay close up by the start line, we were heartened by the sight of 500 heavy bombers streaming in from the coast in a long unswerving line straight over the city. They completely ignored the heavy **flak** and we watched the bombs come streaming down. One aircraft disappeared completely in a huge white flash, another tilted over and spun down, losing a wing on its journey, but a third, obviously in trouble, flew lower and lower in a large circle, and as it passed over us I could see that all the fabric covering the tail and rudder had been shot away. We marvelled at how it kept on flying, and eventually it appeared to come down well behind our lines. Soon the whole target area became obscured by smoke and dust, rising high in the air. But still the bombers roared across. This was a terrific **morale** booster for us, but had little effect on our immediate objective, the village of La Bijude, which was well outside the target area.

Normandy was a region of narrow lanes and patchwork fields bounded by earth banks topped with hedges. This hedgerow country proved to be a great defence aid to the Germans. In this picture British troops shelter from German field-gun fire during the bitter struggle to capture the French city of Caen.

The Battle of Normandy

Throughout July the **Allies** slowly began to make progress against the Germans in what became known as the Battle of Normandy. Hitler, still convinced that a larger Allied invasion was yet to come in northern France, refused to send essential supplies and troops south. The British finally captured the city of Caen, though there was little of it left standing after the heavy allied bombing. Cherbourg and the inland town of St-Lô were already in Allied hands. Now the Allies controlled all of the Normandy Peninsula, from Caen in the north to Avranches in the south (see map page 30). It was time now to break out, and move eastwards against German troops in the rest of France.

US general Omar Bradley began the break-out on 25 July with an attack south from St-Lô. British and Canadian troops moved south and east from Caen. About a week later another US attack moved east from Avranches. The Germans were in retreat, but put up a last valiant effort near the town of Falaise. They held out until 20 August, but then retreated across the River Seine. This allowed Allied troops, along with members of the French **Resistance** and Free French troops to **liberate** Paris on 25 August.

The Normandy town of St-Lô, which blocked the Allied advance from the landing beaches, lies in ruins after weeks of heavy fighting.

Major-General Meyer remembers

Major-General Kurt Meyer had led his German troops from Caen to Falaise in late July 1944. They were part of Germany's last attempt to stop the Allied advance. Here he describes the fighting on 14–15 August 1944 around some high ground given the name Hill 159 by the German army. In September Meyer was captured and handed over to the Americans.

We do not understand the enemy ... His vastly superior numbers of tanks only have to drive over us at full speed to finish us but nothing happens. Each attack is repulsed until the afternoon ... Fighter bombers launch themselves on the little forest of Bois du Roi unleashing their rockets into the long destroyed forest. Some tanks east of Hill 159 fall victim to the Typhoon [fighter plane armed with bombs or rockets] attacks. I meet Max Wünsche [a comrade], between Versainville and Hill 159. He tells me of the now hopeless situation on the hill. Enemy tanks race towards us. Their shells explode on the road, Max Wünsche disappears. I feel a burning hot pain, blood runs across my face, I dive head first into a little hedge, a shell splinter has cut my head open. I look dizzily at the road. Our Kubelwagen [open-topped tank] has disappeared and Max Bornhöft [another comrade] is no longer to be seen. I am alone but at no time do I feel deserted, I know my comrades will not leave me here.

What have we learnt from D-Day?

The D-Day landings of 6 June 1944 were the largest invasion in history. The **Allied** military leaders planned every aspect of the operation and drilled it over and over in the months leading up to Operation Overlord. Soldiers from all over the world were involved. A spirit of determination and co-operation meant that it succeeded despite bad weather and fierce German resistance, and even though things did not always go according to plan. Some have argued that mistakes were made after the five beaches were captured. The grim battles that followed were made worse by a lack of co-ordination among those directing the troops, and in some cases the poor performance of the soldiers. But on both sides the fighting was very fierce. The German troops knew they were fighting for their survival, while Allied troops felt they were fighting for their freedom and the freedom of Europe.

The lessons of this great battle go far beyond providing guidelines for future military operations. Everyone on the Allied side felt that they could play a part in preserving freedom, even if it was the soldiers who might pay the ultimate price – death (roughly 150,000 soldiers, sailors and airmen lost their lives in the Normandy campaign). The planning, efforts and sacrifices of D-Day were crucial and paved the way for the Allied victory in Europe in May 1945. Though terribly costly, in terms of the death and destruction caused, there appeared to be no other way of **liberating** Europe from **Nazi** aggression.

An enduring memorial: a US helmet hangs on a cross marked 'MORT POUR LA FRANCE' (He died for France) in a Normandy cemetery.

Stephen Ambrose remembers how ordinary people felt about D-Day
The US historian Stephen Ambrose, who died in October 2002, was one of the leading experts on D-Day and World War II in general. Here he looks back to his own experiences at the time of D-Day.

One of the features of D-Day is, we were all involved. I was making the contribution that a 10-year-old could make; my mother was making the contribution she could make. Women all over this country were working night shifts in the factories, turning out **munitions** or boots or binoculars or any of the other many items that troops need to go into battle. And then they were working days, volunteers at the Red Cross rolling bandages. When the news came to this country on the morning of June 6 that the invasion had started, there was an overwhelming impulse to go to church or synagogue and pray, and what these people prayed was, 'God, I hope I did it right. The bandages that I rolled, the bullets that I made are going into battle, even as I am here praying. Please, God, let me have done it right.'

Timeline

1939	1 September: Germany invades Poland triggering the start of World War II in Europe.
1940	10 May: Germany invades Belgium and the Netherlands. Winston Churchill becomes the new British prime minister.
	22 June: Germany's victory over France is complete.
1941	22 June: Germany invades the **Soviet Union**.
	7 December: Japan attacks Pearl Harbor.
	11 December: Germany and Italy declare war on the USA.
1942	23 October: General Montgomery wins a victory against the Germans at El Alamein in Eygpt, North Africa. Eisenhower leads the **Allied** forces in Operation Torch in North Africa.
1943	12-25 May: British prime minister, Winston Churchill, meets US president, Franklin Roosevelt, in Washington to discuss the cross-Channel invasion called D-Day.
	3 September: Italy secretly surrenders to the Allies, but Germany controls most of the country.
	9 September: Allied troops land at Salerno, Italy.
	24–29 December: Announcements in London and Washington reveal that General Dwight Eisenhower is to be the Supreme Allied Commander for the D-Day invasion. Admiral Sir Bertram Ramsay and Air Marshal Leigh Mallory will lead the air and naval forces.
1944	6 June: D-Day – Allied troops land in Normandy to begin the invasion in northern France.

Below are the approximate times and sequence of the events of D-Day:

00:00: First airborne troops begin to land.

01:00: Landing craft begin to be lowered into the water; **paratroopers** cut phone lines and knock down telephone poles.

02:00: First bombers take off to attack targets around the beachhead.

03:00: Gliders begin to reinforce paratroopers.

03:09: German radar detects Allied invasion fleet. Admiral Krancke orders shore defences to prepare for invasion.

05:20: Bombers drop first bombs on German targets at sunrise.

05:35: German **artillery** opens fire; Allied naval forces return fire.

06:20: Allied landing craft approach the beaches.

06:30: US troops land at Utah and Omaha Beaches.

07:25: British troops begin to land at Sword Beach.

07:35: British troops land at Gold Beach.

08:00: Canadian troops land at Juno Beach.

08:30: Landing craft begin delivery of armour at Omaha.

10:45: Utah nearly captured; more troops come ashore.

12:00: Gold, Juno and Sword beaches under Allied control.

13:00: Troops at Omaha begin to capture the beach.

16:00: Hitler finally gives approval to release **panzers** to combat Allied invasion, too late to prevent success of the landings.

June, July and August: Battle of Normandy.

25 August: Paris is **liberated** by US and French forces.

Find out more

Books & websites

D-Day Landing Sites, Bob Rees, (Heinemann Library, 2002)
The Causes of World War II, Paul Dowswell, (Heinemann Library, 2002)
20th Century Perspectives: Key Battles of World War II, Fiona Reynoldson,
 (Heinemann Library, 2002)
20th Century Perspectives: Weapons and Technology of World War II, Windsor Chorlton,
 (Heinemann Library, 2002)
World War II on Land, Neil Tonge, (Raintree, 2002)
World War II at Sea, Peter Hepplewhite, (Raintree, 2002)

Go Exploring! Log on to Heinemann's online history resource.
www.heinemannexplore.co.uk

www.ibiscom.com/ww2frm.htm
Eyewitness accounts of World War II from people who were there. Audio links provide
actual newscasts of some of the events.

www.spartacus.schoolnet.co.uk
The Spartacus site, based in Britain, contains a wealth of information about all aspects
of World War II, with information from most countries that were involved.

List of primary sources

The author and publisher gratefully acknowledge the following publications and
websites from which written sources in the book are drawn. In some cases the
wording or sentence structure has been simplified to make the material more
appropriate for a school readership.

P.9 Winston Churchill: www.winstonchurchill.org/ffhmount.htm
P.11 Dean McCandless: www.thedropzone.org/europe/sicily/mccandless.html
P.13 Private Gordon Carson: *The Victors: Eisenhower and His Boys: the Men of World War II*,
    Stephen E. Ambrose (Simon & Schuster, 1998)
P. 15 Teheran statement from Roosevelt, Churchill and Stalin
    www.yale.edu/lawweb/avalon/wwii/tehran.htm
P.17 Guenther Blumentritt: www. normandy.ed.com/normandy
P.19 Brenda Webb: www.orcadian.co.uk/features/
P.21 Alan Moorehead: *Eclipse*: Alan Moorehead (Hamish Hamilton, 1945)
P.23 General Eisenhower: www.spartacus.schoolnet.co.uk/2wwpatton.htm
P.25 Major Hans von Luck: www. normandy.ed.com/normandy/pri/Q00204.html
P.27 General Eisenhower: www.eisenhower.utexas.edu/ssa.htm
P.29 English housewife: *'44: In Combat on the Western Front from Normandy to the Ardennes*:
    Charles Whiting (Century, 1984)
P.31 James Delong: www.normandy.ed.com/normandy
P.33 Sergeant Thornton: www. normandy.ed.com/normandy
P.35 Franz Gockel: *Voices of D-Day: The Story of the Allied Invasion Told by Those Who Were There*:
    Ed Ronald J. Drez. (Louisiana State University Press, 1994)

P.37 J.H. Hamilton: *Voices of D-Day: The Story of the Allied Invasion Told by Those Who Were There*, Ed by Ronald J. Drez. (Louisiana State University Press: 1994)

P.39 William J. Stanley: pearlharbor.military.com/nps_history_oral.html

P.41 Ernie Pyle: *Ernie's War: The Best of Ernie Pyle's World War II Dispatches*. Ed David Nichols (Random House, 1986)

P.43 Private Carlton W. Barrett: http://www.dvrbs.com/110thMedBnTxt10.htm

P.45 Mlle Genget: *The Victors: Eisenhower and His Boys: the Men of World War II*: Stephen E. Ambrose (Simon & Schuster, 1998)

P.47 Lieutenant John Brown www.valourandhorror.com/DB/ISSUE/Liberating–Caen.htm

P.49 Major-General Kurt Meyers: http://search.eb.com/normandy/pri/Q00208.html

P.51 Stephen E. Ambrose: www.c-span.org/mmedia/booknote/ lambbook/transcripts/10005.htm

Glossary

alliance   an agreement between countries to support one another

Allies, or Allied   referring to the countries, including Great Britain, France, the USA and the Soviet Union, which fought against the Axis powers

amphibious   involving activities in water and on land

anti-aircraft   designed to shoot down aircraft

artillery   cannons and other heavy, powerful weapons that cannot be held by one person

Axis   describing the military forces of, and the alliance between Germany, Italy, Japan and the countries that fought with them during World War II

barrage   constant firing of cannons or other artillery

bastion   fortress or any place or institution that is seen to protect some basic quality such as freedom

battery   (in military terms) fortress equipped with artillery

bias   judgement that is clouded by personal opinion

bunker   heavily defended place usually set underground or mainly underground

casualties   people who are killed, wounded or missing in a battle

censorship   removing sensitive military information from letters or newspaper reports during a war

citation   official statement about the reasons for giving an honour

civilian   someone who is not part of an army and not directly involved with fighting

commando   soldier who goes on special, and sometimes secret, mission

conscription   compulsory service in the armed forces

convoy   group of ships or other large vehicles travelling together for protection

decryption   decoding of a coded message

Eastern Front   part of Eastern Europe, mainly the Soviet Union, where Germany fought against Allied forces

flak   exploding anti-aircraft shells

flank   side of a battle area

front   full width of a battle area where two opposing armies meet

garrison   group of troops stationed in a defended place

GI   an abbreviation (widely believed to be 'Government Issue') that was used as a nickname for a US soldier

half tide   the point when seawater is halfway between its deepest (high tide) and its shallowest (low tide)

illusory   false and misleading

impregnable   unable to be defeated or destroyed

54

impulsiveness acting without thinking about the consequences

indiscretion an action that is not based on proper judgement

indoctrinate fill a person's mind with beliefs and ideas that must not be criticized

infantry soldiers on foot

intelligence (in military terms) information gained about the enemy

intrepidity bravery combined with fearlessness

liberate free someone or something

memoirs personal account of an historical event or period

meteorologist scientist who specializes in studying the weather and how it can be predicted

military dictatorship political situation where military leader, or leaders, have total power to rule the country

minefield area of land or sea that is planted with explosive mines

mine-sweepers warships used especially to detect and remove mines laid by the enemy

morale mental state of a person or group of people (whether they are cheerful or confident), usually in times of crisis

Morse code system of dots and dashes representing letters of the alphabet and used to transmit radio messages

munitions weapons and ammunition used in war

Nazi (short for 'National Socialist' in German), the ruling German political party during World War II

NCO (an abbreviation for Non-Commissioned Officer), one of the lowest-ranking officers in the military, such as a corporal or sergeant

opposed landing landing soldiers and equipment along a coastline defended by the enemy

oppressed denied basic rights and freedoms

panzer German tank

paratroopers specially trained soldiers who arrive behind enemy lines by parachute

prejudice fixed belief or opinion formed without a fair examination of the facts

primary source original account describing an historical event or era

reprimand speak severely to someone over some wrongdoing

Resistance secret organization of individuals working to overthrow an occupying force

sabotage destroy or damage something to gain political or military advantage

secondary source second-hand historical account

shrapnel sharp pieces of metal sent flying by an explosion

Soviet Union huge communist country that included Russia. It broke into separate countries in the early 1990s.

strategy overall, long-term planning

tracer bullets or artillery shells that are illuminated to help artillery soldiers aim

tyranny uncontrolled use of power by a government or ruler

War Department department of the US government responsible for defence and military actions during World War II; now part of the Department of Defence

Western Front area of military conflict where the Axis powers faced the Allies in Western Europe

Index

Titles in the *Witness To History* series include:

Hardback   0 431 17044 4

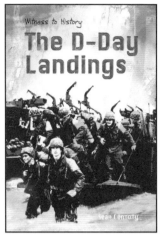

Hardback   0 431 17043 6

Hardback   0 431 17042 8

Hardback   0 431 17034 7

Hardback   0 431 17046 0

Hardback   0 431 17045 2

Find out about the other titles in this series on our website www.heinemann.co.uk/library